Georgia Law requires Library materials to
be returned or replacement costs paid.
Failure to comply is a misdemeanor
punishable by law. (O.C.G.A 20-5-53)

D1405489

BRUNSWICK-GLYNN COUNTY REGIONAL LIBRARY
208 GLOUCESTER ST.
BRUNSWICK, GA. 31520

IDENTIFICATION
CAGE AND

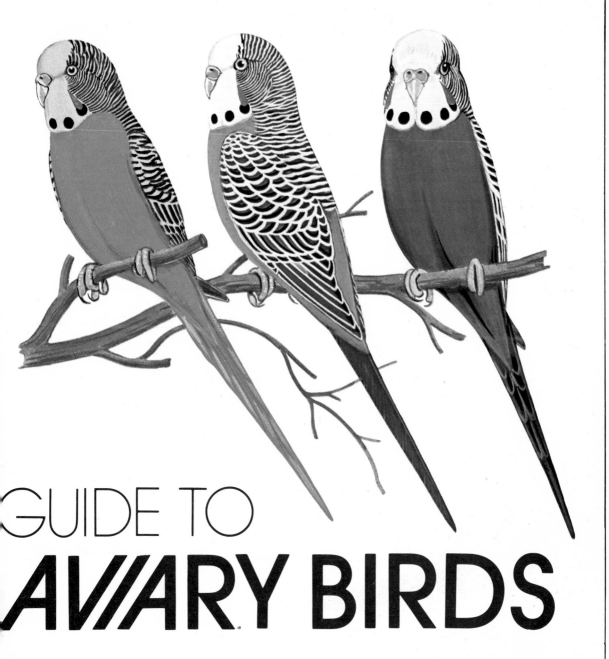

GUIDE TO
AVIARY BIRDS

Written and illustrated by Michael Stringer

ARCO PUBLISHING COMPANY, INC.
New York

636.686
5918i

Published by Arco Publishing Company, Inc.
219 Park Avenue South, New York, N.Y. 10003

Copyright © 1977 by Blaketon-Hall Limited

All rights reserved

No part of this publication may be reproduced,
photocopied, stored in a retrieval system, or
otherwise reproduced without the express
permission of the publishers in writing.

Printed in Great Britain

Library of Congress Cataloging in Publication Data

Stringer, Michael, 1924–
  Identification guide to cage and aviary birds.

  1. Cage-birds—Identification. I. Title. II. Title:
Cage and aviary birds.
SF461.S87   636.6'86   77-4065
ISBN 0–668–04298–2

Contents

Introduction

Many people find birds fascinating so it is rather surprising that more people do not keep birds as a hobby, either to add interest to a garden, provide pleasure in breeding, or simply as household pets. There is a wide variety of interesting birds that the novice can acquire, the majority of them being inexpensive and easy to obtain. Although most birds are not difficult to cater for, they must be provided with the correct type of accommodation if they are to remain healthy, have long lives, and thus give pleasure to their owners. Birds are very active creatures and it is cruel to keep them in cages unless the species acquired is one of those types that is happy in a cage. Budgerigars, Canaries, Goldfinches, and some Parrots are among the species that obviously thrive in cages, but there are others that are quite unsuited to cage life and these must be provided with an aviary. To provide a suitable aviary is no problem and there are a number of bird species that can be kept in a mixed collection which will prove even more interesting to the bird lover.

Buying Birds

Before starting out to buy a bird it is better if one gets as much information as possible on the requirements and feeding of the bird, then set out to obtain that particular bird from a reliable dealer. This is a better way of going about it than simply walking into a pet store and buying the most attractive bird yet not knowing how to keep it. It should not be assumed that all the birds displayed in a pet shop are easy to care for. Many birds are not as easy to care for as the familiar Budgerigar, and will not thrive unless due attention is given to their requirements. The birds should be looked at carefully before they are purchased. A bird should be alert and perky, have a bright eye and a clean vent. The feathers should be neat and trim and the legs and feet clean, without any crooked toes or other malformation.

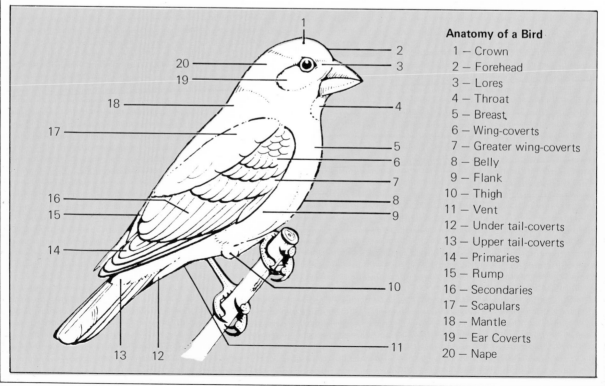

Anatomy of a Bird

1 — Crown
2 — Forehead
3 — Lores
4 — Throat
5 — Breast
6 — Wing-coverts
7 — Greater wing-coverts
8 — Belly
9 — Flank
10 — Thigh
11 — Vent
12 — Under tail-coverts
13 — Upper tail-coverts
14 — Primaries
15 — Rump
16 — Secondaries
17 — Scapulars
18 — Mantle
19 — Ear Coverts
20 — Nape

An unhealthy bird can soon be seen in a group. A bird that sits with feathers puffed out or appears generally listless should not be bought. Having once acquired a bird it must be kept in a quiet place away from other birds in your collection for a few days until it settles down. When introducing it to the aviary it is a good idea to keep the new bird in a cage in full view of the other birds for a day or so for them to become familiar with their new companion. Very often birds will panic at the sight of a new bird, especially if it is brightly colored and chasing and injury might occur before the birds have had long enough to get used to each other. When keeping birds in a mixed collection in an aviary it must be established which birds mix well. The general rule to apply is to keep only birds of similar size together as larger birds often bully smaller species. If a pair of one species is kept with other birds the pair will often become aggressive, in fact when the breeding season comes around most pairs will certainly become aggressive towards others. The larger billed birds, even if they are normally quiet birds, can be a problem at this time since one peck from their beak can easily kill a small bird. Many of the birds offered for sale are wild-caught birds and are therefore nervous of human beings. They must be treated gently and with kindness if they are to settle down in a cage or aviary. When approaching birds one must always give an indication of ones approach by talking gently to the birds in order that they do not take fright at your sudden appearance. Talking gently to birds puts them at ease as they fear silence and in fact one of the great pleasures of bird-keeping is when they become tame and trusting. Despite what has been said regarding the mixing of sizes in birds there are some larger birds that can be safely associated with smaller ones.

It is advisable to buy foreign birds during the summer or spring as they will become acclimatized easier during the warm weather. This must be borne in mind as acclimatization is very important to these small creatures that have been taken from one climate to another in a very short space of time. Some species are of course very delicate and need to be kept in indoor conditions throughout the year, this particularly applies to some of the softbills. The normal daytime house temperature is sufficient for most of these birds. The beginner would be advised to start with hardy birds which are both cheaper and easier to acquire than the more difficult birds. When buying a bird, particularly an expensive one such as a Cockatoo, it must be established that it is a young one. An older bird that has either been caught whilst an adult, or been kept for a long time by another person will not become such a good pet as a young one. If a Parrot is required to be kept simply as a pet it will only become tame and confiding if kept away from others of the same species, and in fact all talking birds must be kept apart from other birds. Singing birds will usually sing more if kept alone. Many of the Parrot family become exceedingly tame; learning to talk, mimic noises, roll around on the carpet, and make friends with the family dog or cat. The Mynah is also a very popular house pet, learning to talk and mimic, although it is a messy feeder and perhaps less suitable for the house than a Parrot. The Amazon Parrots and Conures being better pets for indoors. Budgerigars and Canaries are very popular, and like the Zebra Finch and Bengalese Finch are suitable as cage birds. Many color mutations of these birds have been established which provide a great deal of interest to fanciers. There are many clubs and organizations which exist to cater for those interested in breeding and showing these popular birds.

Head of Cock Cockatiel.

Cages

It is important to think ahead before obtaining birds and advance thought also needs to be given to the type of cage to be used. The cage should be prepared and fitted out before the arrival of the bird or birds. Everyone is familiar with the normal decorative all-wire cage for use in the home, but these are not always suitable for some birds. Budgerigars seem to thrive in them, but nervous and shy birds will not settle down in such a cage. The all-wire cage gives the bird no protection from draughts and allows the bird little privacy. Although at first sight the box cage might appear a little unsightly, it provides a better home for the bird. If it is desired to keep a small collection of birds indoors they should either be kept in separate cages or given a small indoor flight. All parts of the cage must be kept clean and non-toxic paints used in its decoration. Fine and coarse sand should be put on the floor of the cage and this must be changed frequently before it becomes badly soiled. Parrots and cockatoos can be kept in either large parrot cages or on stand perches. The cage should be large enough to allow the bird to stretch its wings and it should be allowed out of its cage every day. To prevent the parrot from flying about the room and perhaps doing damage to ornaments one wing can be clipped annually. Only the large primary feathers of one wing need be cut and this must be done with care as these feathers contain blood vessels near to the base and clipping too short will cause pain and bleeding. The novice should always get professional advice before considering wing-clipping. When letting birds out of their cages care should be taken to see that the birds cannot get their claws caught in net curtains or they may receive injury from broken claws and feet. Stoves and hot surfaces can also be a source of danger to birds. Keep all cages away from direct sunlight, stoves, draughts, etc. A cage put against a draught-free window during warm weather will keep birds amused (especially parrots and Mynahs) when the house is empty, but beware of hot sunshine from which the birds cannot escape.

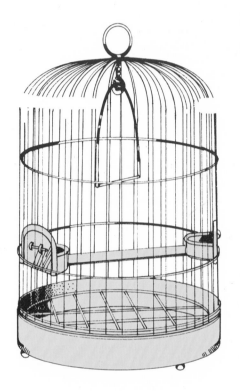

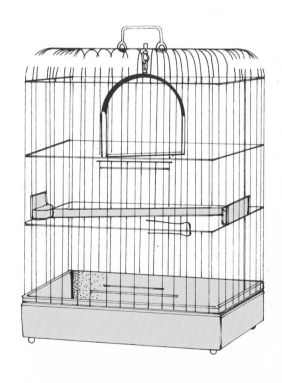

From L to R
Grey Opaline Hen, Grey-Green Hen, Grey Opaline Cock,
Grey Opaline Cock all at six weeks old.

(Cages) Box cage for a pair of small breeding birds such as canaries, Zebra Finches, etc., and also suitable for a pet Mynah. A large parrot cage suitable for a single parrot or cockatoo. A good well made cage must be acquired as a cage made of cheaper materials might poison the bird as parrots tend to nibble the bars.

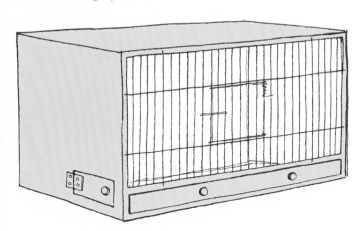

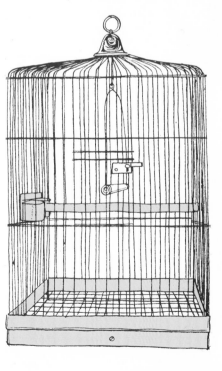

Aviaries

Although the keeping of one or two birds as pets is most enjoyable, many bird lovers will obviously want to keep more, and for this an aviary is usually necessary. It need not be a large or expensive aviary, as quite a small one will house several species. If it is desired that a pair of birds should breed, then this is best done in an aviary, in fact most species will not breed unless given the space and freedom that an aviary provides. A breeding pair should have an aviary to themselves although there are a few birds that will breed in a mixed collection. Many birdkeepers are not so interested in the breeding of birds and will merely wish to keep a small collection for interest.

Before choosing your aviary birds you must establish which birds will mix and stay compatible. An aviary can be a simply-built affair to a plain design, or more lavishly designed to fit into your garden scene. If sited amongst shrubs and trees it will add beauty and interest to the garden. If placed against a wall or fence this will give protection from cold winds. A small portable aviary can be made and moved to a different site each year. This will ensure that the ground area of the flight does not become sour and encourage disease. A permanent aviary is better but the novice should be sure that it is placed in a suitable position so that it will not have to be moved in the future. The aviary should be provided with a concrete floor which can easily be washed down to prevent contamination by the birds' droppings. Shrubs and small trees for the aviary can be kept in movable tubs which can be taken out periodically to be given a rest from the attentions of the birds. In this way, pretty and attractive shrubs can be put in the flight whilst in their best condition. The normal aviary consists of two parts; the shelter and the flight.

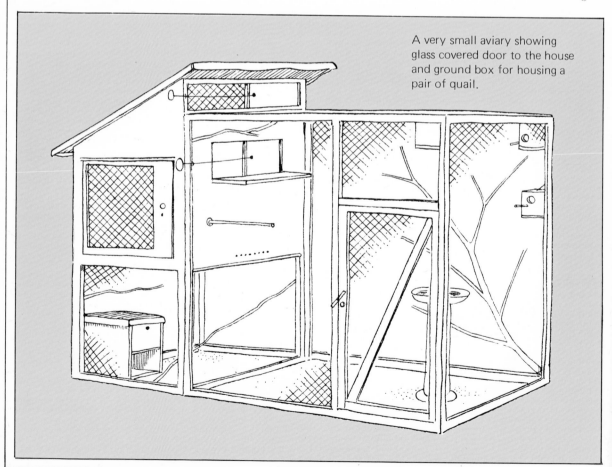

A very small aviary showing glass covered door to the house and ground box for housing a pair of quail.

The flight should be much larger than the shelter. The novice would be advised not to have an aviary that is too small. He or she will quite likely want to add more birds as time goes by and also it can spoil the pleasure of caring for your birds if you constantly get caught-up on woodwork or have to bend double to get inside.

The aviary should be placed where it will receive the maximum amount of winter sunshine. Unless there is a wall or fence behind the aviary it is advisable to have the far side of the flight boarded-up to give protection from bad weather. Half the area of the top of the flight should be covered to make it rainproof. This will not only allow the birds to be outside yet remain dry during wet weather but will also allow some rain to fall into part of the flight as some birds enjoy a shower. Small gauge wire-netting should be used for the aviary. If it is in-

tended to keep parrots then strong chain-link netting fixed to a metal aviary frame will be necessary. Vermin can be a problem with bird-keeping and it is better to extend the wire netting to 6 inches below ground level to keep out rats and mice which are attracted by the bird seed. If a rat were to enter the shelter during the night it would quite likely kill some, if not all of the birds. A concrete floor to the aviary will keep out rats, but mice, being smaller, may get through the wire unless a sheet-metal skirting is fixed around the aviary at ground level. All food and water containers should be placed at a sufficient height to prevent vermin getting at them. The shelter should have adequate ventilation and given protection from draughts and dampness. A double covering of roofing felt will keep the roof watertight. An inlet grille for ventilation should be provided low down, with another

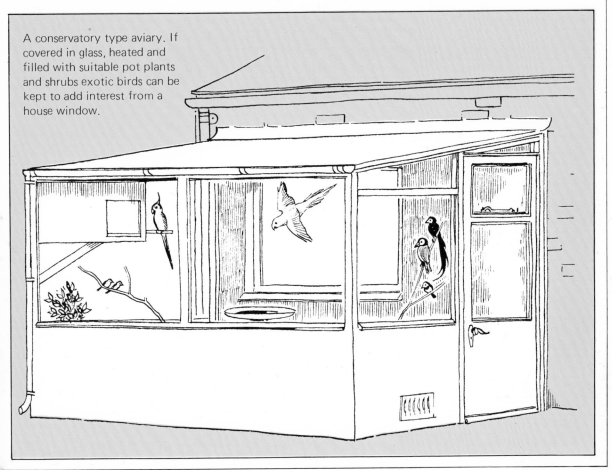

A conservatory type aviary. If covered in glass, heated and filled with suitable pot plants and shrubs exotic birds can be kept to add interest from a house window.

placed in the opposite wall. Provide at least one window in the shelter that can be opened, and cover the glass with wire-netting to make it more visible and so prevent the birds bumping into it and causing themselves injury. Non-toxic materials should be used in the construction of the aviary, and any paints used should not contain lead.

To allow the birds access from the shelter into the flight a very small door, often called the pophole by fanciers, should be incorporated into the structure. This should be positioned high up on the shelter as most birds prefer to enter their quarters at a good height from ground level. The pophole should not be too small as sometimes more than one bird will be going in and out. It can be closed at night by means of a small shutter. The window in the shelter should be large enough to prevent the inside being too dark during the day. If it is found that one or two of the birds are reluctant to enter the shelter at night, this could suggest the presence of a bully amongst the birds. Some birds can be fairly tolerant in the flight but show possessiveness in their use of the shelter. A few very hardy species prefer to roost outside and this should be discouraged, but if the bird persists then be sure there is a cover over the roosting spot to prevent the bird getting soaked during a heavy shower of rain in the night. Perches, nest-boxes, and nest-baskets, together with nesting materials must be provided for the birds inside the shelter, as many species roost inside the nest-boxes. There should be a door from the outside into the shelter, but the door serving the flight must be so arranged that no bird will escape whilst the owner is going in and out of the aviary flight. A large aviary can be fitted with two doors in a porch arrangement, but for a small aviary a small door low down will suffice. Although this means that you have to bend down each time you enter the flight, this is a small penalty to pay for security, since it is unlikely that the birds will fly out as they prefer, when nervous, to fly upwards. It should not be necessary for the owner to enter the flight every day as the water and food dish can be serviced through a small hatchway which can be incorporated into the side of the flight.

A large but shallow receptacle must be provided and filled with clean water each day. Some birds will also use this as a bath. A seed dish or hopper should be provided for the birds in the flight and put well off the ground to prevent vermin getting at it at night. A box of fine sand should be placed on the ground as many birds enjoy a dust bath. The enthusiast will derive great pleasure from his or her mixed collection in the aviary and should take the opportunity to include in the collection a pair of small ground birds such as quail. There are several species to choose from, the Chinese Painted Quail being the most popular. These birds will live amicably with other small birds and provide added interest as they only occupy the ground area of the flight. If the flight has a concrete floor a few turfs can be placed on the ground for the benefit of the quail and other birds, and the grass goes well with the shrubs in tubs. For some species it is essential that there are plants and shrubs in the flight if they are to thrive and breed. It is however pointless to put shrubs into an aviary of parrots or parrakeets, as they will soon tear them to pieces. There are many shrubs to choose from that are suitable and harmless to the birds. Climbing shrubs are of particular interest, as they will provide permanent cover for the birds and provide sites for nesting. Cypress, Cotoneaster, and many berried shrubs are useful for an aviary. If a shrub is grown in a tub or a hole in the concrete floor it can be kept there permanently, but the top couple of inches or so of soil must be replaced every few weeks to prevent contamination by the birds' droppings.

For less hardy birds some form of heating will be required during the winter. This can be provided by an electric tubular heater fixed within the shelter, and thermostatically controlled. Paraffin stoves are not a good idea as they can give off harmful fumes, but in a large, well-ventilated shelter a good brand of stove might be suitable. It would be better to keep really delicate birds in a conservatory-type aviary, where heating can be more readily provided. If the flight is built near the house and within view of a window the owner will have the advantage of enjoying the birds whilst still indoors.

Mixed Collections of Birds for the Aviary

The novice will get great enjoyment in selecting birds for a mixed aviary. As a general rule only birds of similar size will mix but this is not always the case, the Cockatiel being perhaps the best example of a popular and pretty bird that is harmless even to smaller companions. It is a good plan to have in the collection only male birds as this will prevent fighting amongst them when a female is introduced. Sometimes cocks will fight over the ownership of a hen even though they may be of a separate species. It is better to put timid species into the aviary first, and then, when other, more confident birds are put in, the shy one will already know which part of the aviary to go to for a sense of security. Plenty of roosting sites should be available, and the provision of two food dishes will prevent an aggressive bird taking over the food area. When making or buying an aviary, the novice might find it a good idea to build two small aviaries at the same time. The purchase of sufficient wire-netting, wood and cement for two aviaries can often be very little more expensive than buying for only one. Two small aviaries will enable both a collection of larger birds and a collection of smaller birds to be kept. Alternatively, a collection of birds can be kept in one aviary, and a single breeding pair in the other. If the bird lover has a large house, he or she may wish to use a spare room as a bird-room instead of building an outside aviary. Many older houses have a loft room which is very often unused, and perhaps this could be used for a mixed collection or for breeding purposes. A room inside the house would give extra scope to the birdkeeper and would provide the warmth that some delicate species require. A very small mixed collection of birds can be kept indoors by means of a home-made table-like flight. This is a large oblong box-shaped flight standing on legs similar to a table. It can be placed in the corner of a conservatory or garden room.

A very small flight projecting from an attic window. Cage birds will be healthier if given access to fresh air.

Feeding

Most birds are easily fed and their needs simple and inexpensive to provide for. The majority of species that will be kept by the beginner will be seed-eaters or hardbills, as they are popularly known. These can be fed a variety of seeds, most of them thriving on canary seed and millets. Spray millet is enjoyed by most hardbills and is very nutritious. With spray millet some of the husks are also eaten by the birds and these provide them with extra nourishment. Loose millet is simply millet without the husks. If only one or two birds are kept a reliable brand of packet seeds can be bought but if several birds are kept it is more economical to buy seeds in bulk from a reliable seedsman. As well as canary seed many hardbills also enjoy yellow millet and sprouted seeds. If some seeds are sown onto a tray of wet soil they will germinate and these can be given to the birds and will help to keep them healthy. Hemp is enjoyed by hardbills but it should only be given in small amounts. Birds of sparrow size will eat crushed oats and paddy rice. Paddy rice being the natural food of some of the hardbills, including the popular Java Sparrow. Birds of the parrot family feed on a variety of seeds, including sunflower seed. All seeds purchased must be clean and any dust or dirt removed, but seeds from a reliable dealer should already be free of any dirt and fusty seeds. Most hardbills require an occasional insect to supplement their seed diet. A piece of cuttlefish bone is absolutely essential and can be fastened onto the bars of the cage with a clip bought for the purpose. A mineral block should also be provided for the birds. Some birds require a great deal of insect food, these birds are popularly known as softbills and are generally a little more difficult to keep than many hardbills. They can be messy feeders, especially if they are kept indoors in a cage. There are good brands of insect foods

Green foods suitable for birds, left to right: dandelion, chickweed, groundsel, seeding grasses and plantain. These must be given to the birds fresh and clean.

available in packet form from seedsmen to suit different species. As well as this kind of food softbills should be given a certain amount of live insects occasionally. One of the best insect foods is ants eggs, these take a great deal of time to collect but are greatly enjoyed by the birds.

Greenfly are also enjoyed as well as fruit flies and maggots. Maggots can be obtained from anglers' shops, and have the advantage that even if they are eaten in large quantities, they will not upset the bird's digestive system. Birds, especially cage birds, should not be allowed to gorge themselves on insects as this will make them ill. Softbills that are kept in a glass conservatory will enjoy catching flies that pupate from the maggot stage. Mealworms are sometimes bought to feed softbills. These are readily consumed, but if given too many the birds can suffer from liver troubles. The novice would be advised to stick to buying maggots, or gentles as they are sometimes known. Some of the larger softbills should be given a little raw chopped meat and most of these birds enjoy chopped boiled egg. If a jar of seed has a little cod liver oil poured into it and kept for a day or so this can be fed in small amounts to all birds and will provide a useful conditioner and supplement to their diet. This is particularly essential for cage birds. A few species require honey in their diet which can be fed to them after being diluted with water and soaked into a sponge cake, or else given to them in a special feeding bottle obtainable at pet stores. Most birds require green food which is easily obtainable. It should be clean and not collected from roadsides where there is a risk of the leaves being polluted by traffic fumes and dust or cats and dogs. Dandelions, Groundsel, Chickweed, and Plantains are the most suitable green food, as well as lettuce and spinach leaves. Bunches of seeding grasses are also enjoyed by hardbills, especially grasses such as Rye and Poa. Some larger hardbills and British Finches will enjoy berries in season. Fruit is appreciated by some birds and is essential for birds of the parrot family. Apples, pears, grapes, bananas and carrots being enjoyed. All food should be fresh and clean. Food receptacles must be cleaned out regularly. Suitable grit should be available to all birds at all times along with a daily supply of fresh, clean water for drinking.

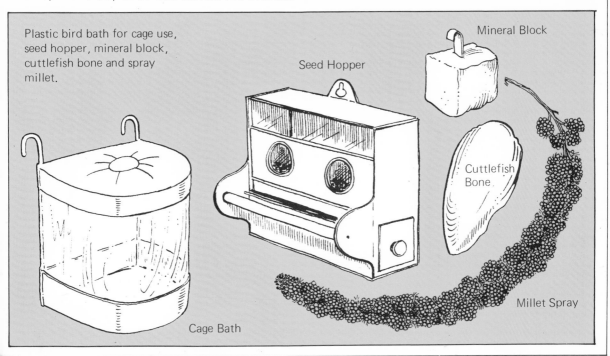

Plastic bird bath for cage use, seed hopper, mineral block, cuttlefish bone and spray millet.

Mineral Block

Seed Hopper

Cuttlefish Bone

Millet Spray

Cage Bath

Breeding

Although there are a great many bird lovers who enjoy keeping birds, many of them are not too interested in breeding them. There are obviously many who simply enjoy their birds for the pleasure they give, either as a caged pet, or as a mixed collection in indoor flight or aviary. But some soon become interested in a particular species and have the desire to breed them. Once an interest in breeding develops, it is advisable for the beginner to contact a local club or society specializing in the chosen bird. There are many such groups which are eager to help with information on birds ranging from Finches, Canaries, Budgerigars, Parrots, Softbills, and Zebra Finches. Many species have still not been successfully bred in captivity and this provides a challenge to the novice and indeed for the professional breeder. In order for a pair to breed they must be given con-

ditions that are as near as possible to those found in the wild. Birds have to mature before they will breed successfully. Some species are mature at a few months old, but others, such as parrots, can only be successfully bred after a number of years. A good clean diet, fresh air, and plenty of freedom are necessary if the birds are to breed. This is especially so for the hen, who must be really healthy in order to breed. With some species it is essential to keep the pair away from other birds or each other outside the breeding season, and to introduce them when the pair are required to breed. With some birds they breed better if kept together for a number of years, particularly parrots. Some birds that are difficult to sex may behave as a breeding pair and only after infertile eggs are laid is it realized that they are two hens and not a cock and hen as hoped. Only an expert

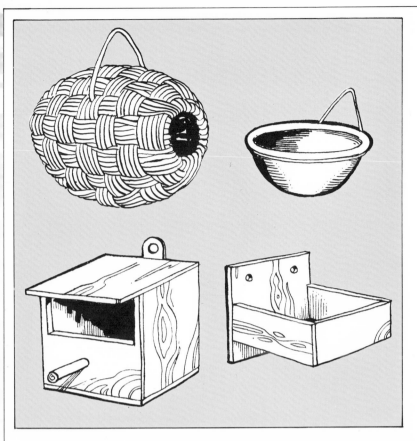

Illustrated here is a nest basket
and open fronted nest box.
Also a nest pan and nest tray
as used by canaries etc.

Photo opposite page:
Gloster Canary, Consort Cock and
Corona Hen.

Photo Below:
Gloster Fancy Canary Hen
and young.

Parrots and cockatoos require a small barrel for nesting. The hollow log nest box is of a smaller size and suitable for most box nesters.

can sex some birds. Of those species where the sexes are alike it is usual for the hen to be slightly smaller than the cock, and of a duller color, although this can also indicate a young cock. Males are usually more aggressive than females, but with some parrots the opposite is usually the case. Lovebirds are often chosen by the novice for breeding. They should have a nest-box and be well supplied with moist bark and fresh twigs. The nest must be kept moist, so lots of damp moss should be provided.

It is possible to breed some birds in a large cage, but most species will not do so unless given an aviary to themselves. Budgerigars, Canaries, Bengalese and Zebra Finches will breed in a large box cage, but an aviary is always better. If cage breeding is attempted it must be in a large cage of box type, and not the fancy all-wire house cage. A breeding aviary for most birds need not be larger than six feet long, but should contain several shrubs as many birds will not breed unless foliage is available. Most birds will prefer to use a nest box or nest basket and several of these should be available to give them a choice of site. A large bunch of heather or gorse fixed against the wire will be better for some birds to nest in. If the birds seem reluctant to build it is a good idea to put some nesting material into some of the boxes to give them a start. In a small aviary most birds will not breed unless separated from other species, and are best kept as one pair without companions. Once breeding has commenced the birds should be disturbed as little as possible and the novice must overcome the desire to look into the nest, as a small amount of disturbance will be enough to make some species abandon the nest completely. Other pets and children must be kept away from the aviary at this difficult period. A good supply of nest materials should be available to the birds and if the novice has any doubt as to which materials the birds will use, a good supply of grass stalks, fresh grass, feathers, cotton, wool, twigs, rootlets, tissue paper, etc. should be sufficient. Most young birds are fed by their parents on insects, and without this food some chicks will quite likely die. The young must be provided with the right kind of food. After the young have left the nest the male might be eager to breed again, and if this behaviour interferes with the hen in the care of the fledglings, then the cock will need to be removed until after the young are independent. He can then be put back, when another brood might appear.

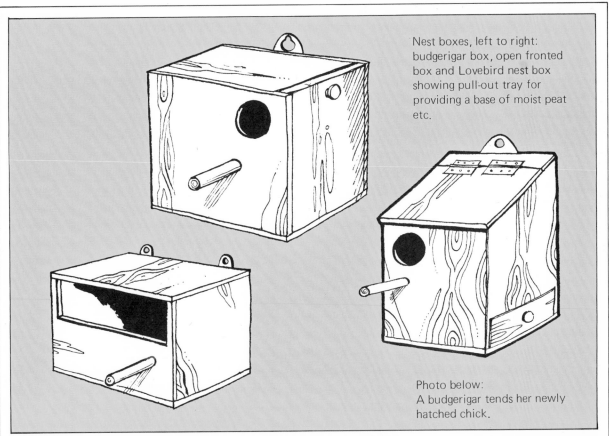

Nest boxes, left to right: budgerigar box, open fronted box and Lovebird nest box showing pull-out tray for providing a base of moist peat etc.

Photo below:
A budgerigar tends her newly hatched chick.

Sickness and Accident

Regardless of the care and attention that the bird-keeper takes with the maintenance of his birds, at some time or other some birds will almost certainly suffer illness or accident. If illness is quickly spotted there should be few problems in effecting a complete cure. Once the novice has become familiar with the birds it will soon become obvious when a bird is unwell. Clean cages and aviaries, fresh water for drinking and bathing, and clean food are essentials in the prevention of sickness. New birds should be kept isolated from others for a couple of weeks, and any sickness which may be carried in a dormant state by the bird should show during that time. A bird which sits with feathers puffed out or eyes closed, or sits by the food hopper without feeding is unwell. Also wet discharge from the vent or irregular breathing are indications of sickness. Such a bird should be taken away from its companions with as little fuss as possible, and put into a hospital cage where the temperature should be maintained between 85° and 90° F. The temperature should be constant. A suitable hospital cage can be home-made, and it will be invaluable in saving the lives of birds that are often only suffering from a temporary chill. Constipation can occur in birds and is usually treated by giving plenty of green food and cod-liver oil. Obviously a veterinarian should be consulted if a valued pet is ill. Over-grown claws can be a problem, these should be snipped off with sharp nail clippers taking care not to cut too short as this will sever the blood vessels which can be seen when the claw is held up to the light. A large rough stone in the cage or aviary will also help prevent the beak becoming overgrown, as the birds will peck at it to keep their beak in shape.

Parasites can sometimes occur if birds are not kept in clean conditions. Perches and corners in cage and aviary should be looked at regularly for Red Mite which will live in these places during the day, emerging only at night to cause irritation to your stock. Should an attack of Red Mite occur, perches, cages, and aviaries should be scrubbed with hot water and when dry brushed over with paraffin. This will kill these pests. The bird-keeper should be on the constant lookout for Red Mite. Caged parrots are often seen in a deplorable condition when not looked after properly. These are very intelligent birds and need company and amusement. They should be let out of their cages as often as possible and given pieces of wood to chew and play with, otherwise they might start to feather pick, which is the aviary equivalent of nail-biting in humans. They must be talked to and regarded as part of the family if they are to remain healthy. Suitable grit must be available for all birds, as well as water for bathing.

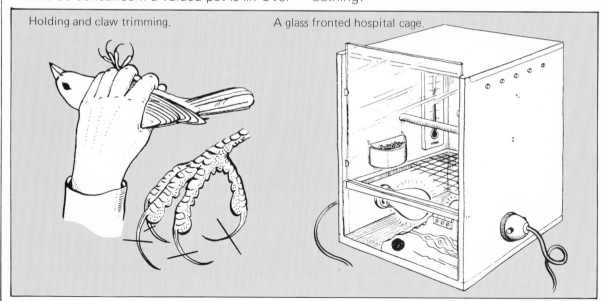

Holding and claw trimming.

A glass fronted hospital cage.

The correct way to hold a small bird, firmly but gently, and where to clip overgrown claws.

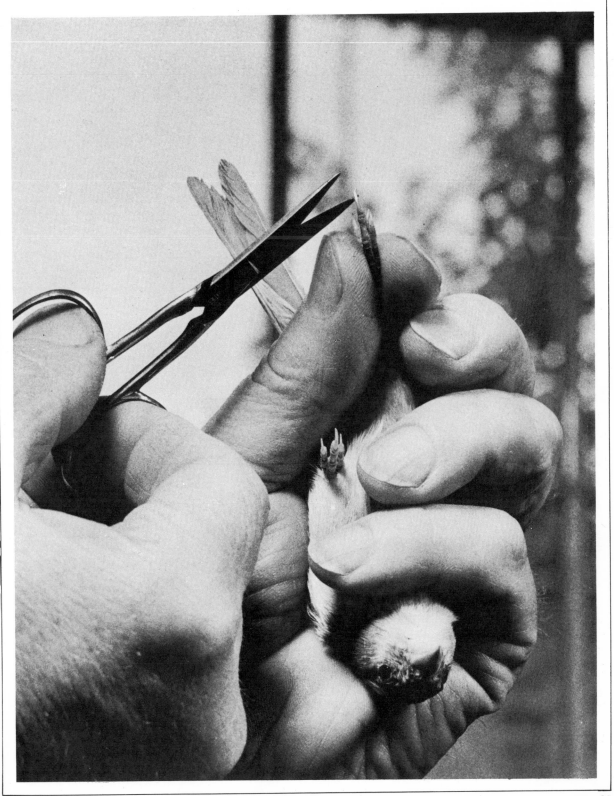

Identification Guide

Golden-Mantled Rosella

Golden Mantled Rosella   15"   37 cm

These birds are recommended to the novice as they are not difficult to keep and are very hardy. They should have an aviary to themselves if breeding is wanted and given a large nest-box placed in an elevated position. The young are fed as parents on canary seed, millets, oats, sunflower seed, buckwheat, hemp and fruits. Also fresh twigs of Hawthorn and apple for the birds to nibble. Sexes alike but the female is not so brightly colored.

Red-Rumped Parakeet

Red-Rumped Parakeet   12"   30 cm

The most popular Australian Parakeet after the Budgerigar. Females lack the red rump and are not so brightly colored. They are excellent birds for the beginner, being hardy and ready breeders. Sometimes mix well but can be aggressive toward smaller birds. A large nest-box in a roomy aviary should induce a pair to breed. Young birds fed as the adults on canary seed, hemp, millets, spray millets, oats, sunflower seed, green food and fruits.

Important Note; Hardy Birds

The text refers to moderate winter conditions. Where severe weather occurs protection and heating will be required even for some so-called hardy species.

Plum-Headed Parakeet   14"   35 cm

Once acclimatized these exceedingly beautiful parakeets are hardy during the winter in a mixed collection of similar size birds. They are quiet birds, the call notes being quite pleasant. The female has similar plumage to the male, the head being blue-grey. A breeding pair should be kept alone and quiet but they are not easy birds to breed. A large nest-box is required, lined with sawdust. Feed the adult birds millets, canary seed, sunflower seed, nuts, apple and spray millet etc.

Plum-Headed Parakeet

Turquosine Grass Parakeet   8"   20 cm

Exceedingly beautiful birds, females not so brightly colored as the males. They are recommended for the novice, being hardy during the winter and quite easy to breed. A large aviary is required as they make great use of their wings. A large nest-box should be provided for breeding. The chicks are fed on a diet of sprouted seeds, seeding grasses and honey soaked in bread. The adults feed on canary seed, oats, hemp, millets, sunflower seed, green food and fruits.

Turquosine
Grass Parakeet

BRUNSWICK-GLYNN COUNTY REGIONAL LIBRARY
208 GLOUCESTER ST.
BRUNSWICK, GA. 31520

Cockatiel

Fischer's Lovebird

Lovebirds 6" 15 cm

Both species of Lovebirds illustrated are easy to keep by the novice, these two being the most popular Lovebirds. They can be kept with other small birds only if a large aviary is provided, and a breeding pair should be kept to themselves. They are only happy if kept as a pair, a single bird being unhappy on its own. They are difficult to sex and often what has been thought of as a devoted pair simply turns out to be two of the same sex. A nest box should be provided and it is most important that the nest is kept moist, the adults must be given fresh twigs from which they will peel the moist bark for nesting material. Breeding can be difficult, but with care, privacy and the precise conditions provided, it can be done. They are very hardy birds outside, but cannot stand damp conditions in winter. A pair can be kept as house pets in a large box-cage provided with plenty of branches. As with all birds, suitable grit and fresh water should always be available. Feed as parakeets.

Cockatiel 13" 32 cm

These kinds are amongst the most popular of parakeets, being ideal mixers and completely inoffensive to smaller companions. They are quiet birds, fairly cheap and soon become tame. If kept alone in a large cage can be taught to mimic. The Cockatiel is perfectly hardy outside and if undisturbed a pair will breed, if provided with a large nest box. The young and adults fed as other small parakeets. Sexes similar, the hen having a yellow tail.

Masked Lovebird

Senegal Parrot

Indian Ring-necked Parakeet

Indian Ring-necked Parakeet 14″ 35 cm
These hardy parakeets have probably been kept as pets longer than any other parakeet as they are thought to have been first introduced to Europe by the Romans. Suitable for a mixed collection, a pair for breeding should be kept separate as the Plum-Headed Parakeet. Fed on sweet fruit, hemp, canary seed, sunflower seed, millets, the young should also be given rusks soaked in milk. If kept alone these birds will learn to talk.

Senegal Parrot 10″ 25 cm
Small, hardy and attractive parrots that are recommended as they are not difficult to keep but can sometimes be noisy. One kept alone as a cage pet will learn to talk, but they are not such ready talkers as some other parrots. They are not ready breeders, but if breeding is attempted they should be provided with a large nest-box. The chicks are fed as the adults on canary seed, millets, sunflower seed, ground nuts, green food and fruits. The sexes are alike.

African-grey Parrot

Lesser Sulphur-Crested Cockatoo

African Grey Parrot   14"   25 cm   Lesser Sulphur-Crested Cockatoo   14"   35 cm

These two birds have been popular for many years as family pets, both being similar in their requirements. Both are excellent talkers and valued as household pets, where they are usually kept in cages or on stands. They should be allowed out of their cages as often as possible for exercise and given wooden objects to prevent boredom. The parrot can sometimes give a nasty bite, the cockatoo tending to be more gentle. These birds are difficult to breed and will not do so until several years old. If breeding is attempted a pair must be provided with a warm metal-lined shelter with a flight built of heavy chain-link netting as they are exceedingly destructive. A large heavy nest box such as an old barrel lined with wood chips and peat can be provided. Young are fed on soaked bread, hard-boiled egg, boiled maize, etc. Adult birds feed on sunflower seed, canary seed, buckwheat, nuts, hemp, green food, carrots and fruit. Those interested in keeping these large parrots would be advised to contact a society devoted to the keeping of these birds.

Yellow-Headed Conure

Yellow-Naped Amazon Parrot

Yellow-Headed Conure   12"   30 cm

These beautiful birds can be kept in a mixed aviary with similar species. They are not difficult to breed but as with others of the parrot family it would be wiser for the novice to start breeding with cheaper and easier birds such as Cockatiels in order to gain experience. Excellent as a family pet if kept indoors. They become very tame and affectionate and will soon learn to talk. Advice should be sought of experienced parrot keepers before purchasing parrots. Feed as the African Grey Parrot. Sexes alike.

Yellow-Naped Amazon Parrot   15"   37 cm

One of the best birds for talking ability and is very gentle and friendly, being the ideal parrot. They become exeedingly affectionate and loyal, play with the family dog or cat and live for many years. Breeding is not advised to the novice but otherwise their needs are the same as the African Grey Parrot. A parrot must be kept away from other parrots in order to become a tame pet and learn to talk, and must be acquired whilst still young. Feed as African Grey Parrot. Sexes alike.

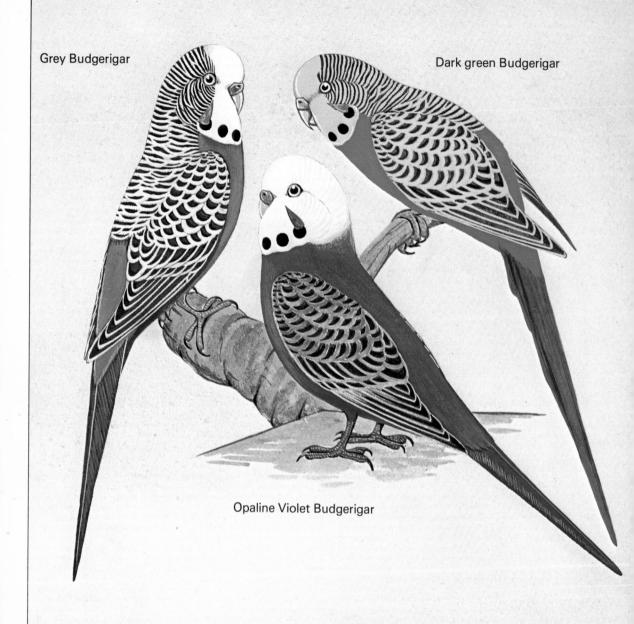

Grey Budgerigar

Dark green Budgerigar

Opaline Violet Budgerigar

Parakeets (Budgerigars)

The Parakeet is undoubtedly the most popular cage and aviary bird, which is not surprising as it is so easy to cater for. They were first introduced from Australia in 1840 and have since been transformed by fanciers from the sober uniform green of the wild bird into the many color variations that are familiar to everyone. New color mutations appear from time to time and it is this factor that has established the Parakeet amongst birdkeepers. Wild Parakeets are still common in their native land, the name Budgerigar (Parakeet) coming from the language of the Australian 'Aborigines, being "betcherrygah" — "good to eat". The first color mutations were yellows which appeared in the 1870s. Much later the familiar blue and other colors appeared. Unlike the canary parakeets have kept their original shape although several crested breeds have appeared.

Yellow-wing Dark Green Budgerigar

Lutino Budgerigar

Opaline Blue Budgerigar

Parakeets (Budgerigars)

The Budgerigar or Parakeet is in great demand as a cage pet and is ideal for this purpose, being intelligent, lively, colorful, easy to care for, and usually a good talker, if given the correct care. Any color bird can learn to talk, the best for this purpose is a young cock. It should be kept away from other budgies and preferably taught to mimic by one person only. Constant talking is required to get the bird to mimic. Those interested in acquiring a Budgerigar as a talking pet would be advised to contact a reliable breeder. It should be kept in a suitable cage well away from draughts and because of this problem the box cage is better for your pet bird. Keep the cage away from fumes and strong sunlight and allow the bird out of the cage as often as possible. The favorite method of bathing for a budgie is to be allowed to stand under a slow flowing tap.

Cobalt Budgerigar

Violet Budgerigar

Light Green Budgerigar

Parakeets (Budgerigars)

As well as being very popular as a cage bird the Budgerigar is the most in demand for the breeder. Breeding can be accomplished either in a cage of the large box type or in an aviary with other pairs. A nest-box should be provided but not nesting materials as these are not required. If young of a particular color are required then obviously the correctly chosen parents should be kept to themselves. Budgerigars tend to be pugnacious so should not be mixed with smaller birds in the aviary, but other parakeets such as Cockatiels and Red-rumped Parakeets can be kept as companions. The novice who wishes to breed budgerigars is advised to contact a local fanciers club where advice can be sought on this interesting hobby. These birds thrive on canary seed, millets, spray millet, and green food.

Canaries

Canaries have been in great demand as cage birds for over three hundred years and along with the Budgerigar are the most popular birds to be kept as pets. There are many varieties suitable either as cage pets or for breeding purposes, including the Norwich, Cinnamons, Yorkshire, Borders, Glosters, Lizards, Frills, Cresteds, Lancashires, and Fifes, etc. All these special breeds are suitable as cage pets, the cocks being valued for their singing qualities. The finest singer is the Roller Canary, which came originally from Germany.

Yorkshire Canary — One of the most popular canaries is the long bodied Yorkshire. These are excellent for the novice breeder to specialize in as they are much in evidence at shows. They are available in a variety of shades, clear yellow, buff, greens, etc. Many breeders feed their birds with color food in order to improve a required color bird, but with the Yorkshire this can be done without the use of color food. Several clubs exist to promote interest in the Yorkshire canary.

Gloster Canary

Yorkshire Canary

Gloster Corona — The Gloster Canary is a bird of recent origin and first appeared in England in about 1925 at the Crystal Palace Show. They are small birds and should not exceed $4\frac{3}{4}$ inches in length. The Gloster Consort is the plainheaded variety and a bird of each type should be used when breeding. The colors range from buff to yellow. Clubs and organizations exist for the Gloster fancy so those interested in breeding with these pretty little birds should contact a local society.

Canaries

Several new color varieties of canary have been developed over the past few years which are of particular interest as cage pets. These include such breeds as the Ivory pastels, Rose Pastels, Apricots, and Red Orange. An all-wire cage is suitable for a canary, although as with a Budgerigar, the box cage is more comfortable, especially as the canary tends to be a nervous bird when compared to the Budgerigar. Because of this anyone wishing to buy a cage bird for the home might do better to buy a Budgerigar unless they have a distinct liking for the canary.

Rose pastel Canary

Cinnamon Buff Canary

Lizard Canary—These are extremely interesting birds, known as lizards because of their somewhat lizard-like plumage pattern and colors. There are many types of lizard, both gold and silver capped. Unfortunately lizards do not keep their true colors and after two or three years are not suitable for the show bench. Birds of lizard-like plumage are obviously not as popular for cage pets as other color canaries but are interesting nonetheless.

Although canaries are popular and familiar birds it should not be assumed that they are easy to breed. They are by nature timid birds and have to be looked after very carefully if breeding is to take place. Breeding stock should be bought during the autumn when there is usually a surplus for sale. A reliable breeder must be contacted if the novice is to make a good start in the hobby of canary breeding.

Lizard Canary

Canaries

Self-green Border Yellow Canary

The breeder of Canaries will often wish to cross his birds with other species of finch to produce different colors. Canaries are bred with success with others such as the Goldfinch, Greenfinch, Bullfinch, Linnet, and Siskin. This provides added interest to the canary lover and as canary keeping is a popular hobby there is no shortage of other enthusiasts to give advice to the novice. These crosses are popularly known as mules and much depends on the interest and patience of the breeder in order for successful breeding to take place.

It is sometimes difficult for the novice to know when to start breeding. Both birds must be in the peak of condition in order for successful breeding to begin. The cock will usually be found singing quite a lot when he is in breeding

Red-orange Canary

Clear Norwich Buff Canary

form and the hen will obviously respond by calling and carrying bits of nesting material in her beak. The vent of the hen will appear slightly swollen. One must take great care at this time not to frighten the birds too much and examination of them must be done carefully.

The breeding pair should be given a large box cage with a wire partition between so that after mating the birds can be separated if need be and also keep them separate until acquainted with each other. If mating is successful a round plastic nest pan with a lining of felt should be provided plus materials for nest building. The chicks are fed on soft foods by the hen and at this time the birds should not be disturbed. Feed all canaries on canary seed, millets and green food.

Goldfinch 5" 12 cm

Ideal as a cage pet as it is quickly tamed, and the cock sings beautifully. The goldfinch will breed quite freely in a large cage or aviary and enjoy the company of other finches. A neat little nest is built of cobwebs, grasses, feathers, etc. Chicks fed as other finches, adults on finch mixture, seeding grasses, etc. Often cross-bred with other finches and canaries, but this seems rather pointless as no prettier bird than the goldfinch could be imagined. Sexes alike.

Goldfinch

Bullfinch

Bullfinch 6" 15 cm

Another pretty finch which is popular with bird fanciers. The song is not of great distinction but they become tame in a cage or aviary. They are however sometimes aggressive towards other small birds. Very good parents and free breeders even in a large cage. The nest is composed of rootlets, small twigs, hair and feathers, the chicks fed on seeding grasses and insects. Adults thrive on a diet of seed mixture, berries, fruit tree buds and a few insects.

Yellowhammer

Yellowhammer 6" 15 cm

This familiar wild bird is not often kept by bird-lovers, not being as popular as some of the other British hardbills. If a mixed collection of birds is aimed for then the Yellowhammer should be included. It is a rather difficult bird for the novice to breed but otherwise requires the same treatment as the Goldfinch, building the nest of grasses nearer the ground. British hardbills are very much neglected in favour of foreign birds, but a mixed flight of native finches is very attractive. Feed as the Chaffinch.

Chaffinch

Chaffinch 6" 15 cm

Not kept as often as other finches but an attractive bird, the hen being of a duller shade. Best kept in an aviary associated with other small birds. Breeding similar to the Linnet, the nest built within the foliage of a shrub. Does not have a distinctive song. Fed on seed mixture, fruit tree buds, berries and as other finches should be given whenever possible seeding grasses, seeding weeds, and insects.

Siskin 5" 12 cm

A pretty little bird, the hen being duller in plumage than the cock. They have very much the characteristics of blue tits, being active and perky, thriving in a mixed aviary or large cage. Siskins are free breeders and their nesting requirements are similar to the goldfinch. Seed mixtures are the staple diet of these birds as well as green food and a few small insects. The cock has a very pleasant song.

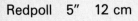

Siskin

Redpoll 5" 12 cm

This little finch is similar in habits to the Siskin, the two species invariably associating together in the wild. Included in a mixed collection of small birds they look very attractive if accommodated in an aviary planted with mature and native shrubs and trees such as Alder, Pine and Spruce. Breeding and feeding care: as the Siskin.

Redpoll

Parson Finch

Combassou

Parson Finch   4"   10 cm

These birds are good breeders but a pair
should not be mixed with other small birds. A
nest-box should be provided with plenty of
grass, rootlets, hairs and feathers. They are
hardy but should not be allowed outside during
the winter months. Feed on millets, small
canary seeds, insects and seeding grasses,
young fed on insects and sprouted seeds.
Sexes similar.

Star Finch   5"   12 cm

One of the most popular and easily bred of the
Australian grass finches. Hardy but should not
be subjected to very cold or damp conditions.
Can be bred in cages or an aviary, nest-box,
grasses, rope shreds, etc. provided. Unless
breeding is desired these pretty birds can be
kept in a mixed collection. Feed on small
canary seed, millets, spray millet, green food,
etc. Sexes similar but the hen not so brightly
colored.

Gouldian Finch   5"   12 cm

One of the most beautiful of all birds, the sexes
being similar. There are also Black-headed and
Yellow-headed forms. They mix well in an
aviary but if breeding is desired they should be
provided with a warm flight indoors. Those
wishing to breed these popular birds would be
advised to join a local Gouldian Finch Society
or Club. Feed plain canary seed, millets, panicum, spray millet and green food.

Combassou   5"   12 cm

These birds are similar to the Whydahs in
habits. The cock out of breeding plumage is
brown as is the female. They are difficult to
breed but when successful will usually deposit
their eggs in the nest of another bird, preferably that of the Melba Finch or other waxbill. Suitable for a mixed collection or as cage
birds, the black plumage of the cock is very
attractive in contrast to others in a collection.
Feeding requirements as the Whydahs.

Star Finch

Diamond Sparrow 4½" 11cm

A pretty Australian weaverfinch which will breed freely in an aviary and is a good bird for a mixed collection, being hardy and quiet. For breeding a nest box should be provided plus grasses and fine roots and feathers for nest building. The young are fed insects, hard boiled egg, green food and sprouted seeds. The adults are fed as the chicks plus millet and canary seed. These birds should be kept in an aviary and are unsuitable for cage life. Sexes alike.

Zebra Finch 4" 10 cm

This is the ideal bird for the novice being easy to keep, breed and mix with other small birds. They are also hardy and there are several domesticated forms to choose from. Hay and dry grasses along with a choice of nest-boxes should be followed by breeding. Chicks are fed sprouted seeds, adults on canary seed, panicum, millets, spray millet, etc. The beginner would be advised to contact a local Zebra Finch society if breeding is hoped for.

Diamond Sparrow

Gouldian Finch

Zebra Finch

Cuban Finch   4″   10 cm

Pretty tit-like finches and easily obtainable. They should not be mixed with other small birds but are nonetheless very attractive. During nesting time they may be allowed to fly at liberty in the garden where they will find natural food for the young. Provide a nest-box and grasses, feathers, etc. The parents should not be disturbed during breeding. Feed on a diet of seeds, weed seeds, seeding grasses, etc. Insect food and ants eggs for the young. Sexes similar.

Cuban Finch

Cut-throat Finch

Cut-throat Finch   5″   12 cm

Excellent birds for the beginner. They can be kept in an outside aviary all winter in a mixed collection, although some individuals are aggressive towards smaller companions. Can sometimes be persuaded to breed if fully acclimatized. The nest is built of dry grasses, rootlets and small feathers. For the chicks the parents should be given sponge cake soaked with honey, small insects and insect mixture. Adult birds fed as Black-headed Nun. The hen lacks the red throat.

Green Singing Finch   4″   10 cm

An ideal cage and aviary bird, the cock noted for his beautiful song. Can be aggressive towards other small birds. A pair will breed in an aviary or cage provided with an open fronted nest-box: hemp and wool for materials. Sometimes a pair will produce a second brood. The young are fed on sprouted seeds, soft food, green foods, grubs, maggots, etc., the adults fed on plain canary seed, yellow panicum, millets, green food and apple. Can live for as long as twenty years. Sexes similar.

Green Singing Finch

Melba Finch   5″   12 cm

Not an easy bird to obtain. Female less bright than the male. They must be carefully acclimatized and are best kept in an indoor flight, where they can be mixed with other birds, although the cock can be aggressive at breeding time. Breeding these birds is difficult but can sometimes be done if given a planted flight to themselves. The nest of dried grasses, hay and rootlets, feathers, etc. is built in an open-fronted nestbox or shrub. Young fed on insects, adults fed as Sydney Waxbill.

Melba Finch

Red-Eared Waxbill

Red-Eared Waxbill   4″   10 cm

The sexes similar, the cock being a brighter color. Interesting little birds and ideal for the beginner, where they can be kept in a mixed collection but are easily frightened. Given a nest-box in an undisturbed corner they will build a beautiful nest: materials including wool and hair. Place several nest-boxes in the aviary to give them a choice of site. The young are fed on ants eggs, egg food and soaked seeds. Adults fed as Green Avadavat.

Sydney Waxbill

Sydney Waxbill   4″   10 cm

A popular Waxbill, quite hardy but requiring heated housing during the winter. They live well in a mixed collection and will usually breed in an aviary after acclimatization. A bottle-shaped nest of grasses, rootlets, hair and wool is built inside a shrub or bunch of heather. The chicks are fed as the young Red Avadavat. The adult birds feed on millets, spray millet, canary seed, seeding grasses and small insects. Sexes similar.

Golden-Breasted Waxbill

Golden-Breasted Waxbill 4" 10 cm

A hardy little Waxbill, ideal for the beginner in a mixed aviary, where it will require some degree of heating at night during the winter. They will often breed if given a small aviary to themselves planted with shrubs. Nests and nesting materials as the Melba Finch. As with most small birds the eggs hatch after about fourteen days, both parents brooding the eggs. Fed on small insects and sprouted seeds, adults as Green Avadavat. Sexes similar, female paler in color.

Lavender Finch

Lavender Finch 5" 12 cm

Ideal birds for a mixed aviary, quickly becoming tame and having a perky tit-like behaviour and a pleasant voice. Although not hardy only one pair of this species should be kept in the aviary as they have the habit of picking each others feathers. Will readily nest in a dark nest-box or shrub using a great deal of nesting materials. Feed the adults and chicks as the Cordon Bleu. Can be allowed liberty during nesting time as the Cuban Finch.

Orange-Cheeked Waxbill

Orange-Cheeked Waxbill 4" 10 cm

Pretty little birds, easily obtainable although rather shy and timid with active tit-like movements. Hardy once acclimatized in a mixed aviary. They might be induced to breed in a nest basket or shrub in the aviary, but are not very free breeders and dislike being disturbed when nesting. The young are fed on small insects while the adults thrive on a diet of millets, spray millet, green food and canary seed. The sexes are similar, the hen having less orange on the cheek.

Linnet

Linnet 5" 12 cm

Traditionally regarded as one of the sweetest singers, the linnet has been popular for many years, both for its song and pretty plumage which is warm brown and crimson in the cock, although the hen is dull brown. Their breeding requirements are similar to the goldfinch, the nest being built in a shrub. The feeding requirements are the same as for the goldfinch, with which it can be kept in a mixed aviary.

Greenfinch 6" 15 cm

Fairly popular hardbills which breed freely, there being several domesticated color variations of the wild bird. Breeding requirements similar to other finches. They are sometimes kept as cage pets, having a pleasant song, but are more frequently kept in a mixed aviary where they can sometimes be aggressive towards smaller birds. Feed seeds, fruit, berries, green food, sunflower seeds and occasionally insects. The hen is of a much more sombre color than the cock.

Greenfinch

Hawfinch

Hawfinch 7" 17 cm

The Hawfinch is not so popular as some other finches, but is interesting nonetheless. It is larger than other kinds in this group and should not be in a mixed collection of smaller birds. The hen is a paler brown shade. Nesting requirements similar to the Bullfinch, although not such a ready breeder. The cock has pleasant call notes but is not such a songster as the Linnet. Food includes kernels of Hawthorn, Beech, Cherry and Sloe, etc. Peas are enjoyed as well as seeds.

Green Cardinal

Japanese Hawfinch

Green Cardinal 8″ 20 cm

Not so bright as other cardinals but very attractive and hardy, not requiring heat but disliking dampness. Outside the breeding season can be kept with birds of the same size in a planted aviary, although pairs are likely to be aggressive towards others. Kept alone a pair will breed in a shrub or open nest-box. Young fed on green food, insects and sprouted seeds, adults on canary seed, millets, sunflower seeds and insects. Sexes similar.

Japanese Hawfinch 8″ 20 cm

These large attractive finches are easy to keep in a mixed collection and are quite hardy outside, not requiring heat during the winter. A planted aviary suits them best where a pair are likely to breed if provided with a nest-box or basket placed in a shrub. The young are fed on small insects, canary chick food, etc., the adults on canary seed, hemp, buckwheat, sunflower seed, insects and green food. The sexes are similar, but the female is of duller plumage.

Red-Crested Cardinal

Hecks' Grassfinch

Virginian Cardinal

Red-Crested Cardinal 8" 20 cm

These popular birds are easily obtainable and can be mixed with smaller birds in a large aviary or with birds of their own size. They are however very pretty, and worth keeping in a small flight on their own where breeding will hopefully take place. The nest is built in a shrub or nest basket provided with grass blades and heather etc. The chicks are fed insects, insect food, egg food, ants eggs, etc. Adults thrive on insects and insect food as the young. Sexes similar.

Virginian Cardinal 9" 22 cm

Very beautiful birds, unfortunately their color becomes less brilliant after moulting in captivity. The plumage of the hen is brown. The cock has a powerful song, often singing at night. Preferably kept alone as a pair they are quite hardy. Provide the birds with several open-fronted nest-boxes high up amongst cover where they might well breed. The chicks are fed entirely on insects, the adults fed on canary seed, millets, hemp, sunflower seeds, fruits, green food and insects.

Hecks' Grassfinch 6" 15 cm

Neat and sleek birds, sexes similar, female having a smaller bib. Should be provided with heat and kept indoors during the winter, otherwise hardy. They tend to be aggressive towards others especially during the breeding season, so are best kept alone in a pair. Several nest-boxes should be provided in the aviary, the chicks are fed on sprouted seeds, insects, etc. The adults fed a diet of plain canary seed, millet spray, millets, green food, and seeding grasses.

Fischers' Whydah

Fischer's Whydah   12"   30 cm

These are very difficult birds to breed and as other Whydahs are parasitic on the nest of other birds, in this case the host bird is the Purple Grenadier Waxbill or Red-Eared Waxbill. Very aggressive towards other birds the cock should be kept with several hens in an aviary. They can be kept outside during the winter but cannot stand frost. Feed as Pintailed Whydah.

Bicheno Finch

Bicheno Finch   4"   10 cm

A very shy bird that is easily frightened, having very much the mannerisms of tits and should be kept in an aviary, where they are most likely to breed, either in the open or a nest-box. Wool and feathers should be supplied for nest building. The chicks are reared on hard-boiled eggs, ants eggs, mealworms, a little cod liver oil and honey. They can be kept in a mixed collection of small birds. Sexes alike.

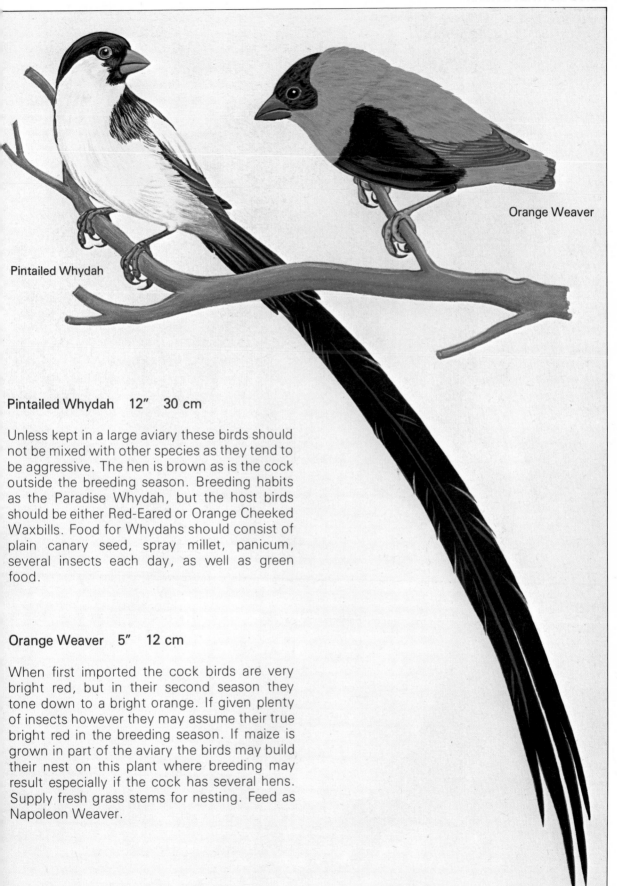

Orange Weaver

Pintailed Whydah

Pintailed Whydah   12″   30 cm

Unless kept in a large aviary these birds should not be mixed with other species as they tend to be aggressive. The hen is brown as is the cock outside the breeding season. Breeding habits as the Paradise Whydah, but the host birds should be either Red-Eared or Orange Cheeked Waxbills. Food for Whydahs should consist of plain canary seed, spray millet, panicum, several insects each day, as well as green food.

Orange Weaver   5″   12 cm

When first imported the cock birds are very bright red, but in their second season they tone down to a bright orange. If given plenty of insects however they may assume their true bright red in the breeding season. If maize is grown in part of the aviary the birds may build their nest on this plant where breeding may result especially if the cock has several hens. Supply fresh grass stems for nesting. Feed as Napoleon Weaver.

Paradise Whydah

Napoleon Weaver

Napoleon Weaver   5"   12 cm

Hardy and easy to keep, one of the most beautiful of the weavers. The plumage of the hen is brown as is the cock outside the breeding season. If breeding is desired it is better to keep several hens with one cock and not mixed with other species. They should be fed on millet, plain canary seed, green food and several maggots each day. Insects are essential if the bright plumage of the male is to be maintained.

Paradise Whydah   20"   50 cm

This is a very popular Whydah which should be kept in an aviary where its pretty display flight can be seen to advantage. The plumage of the hen is brown as is that of the cock outside the breeding season. They are quite friendly towards other birds but can be aggressive during nesting time, when the hen has the habit of laying her eggs in the nests of other birds such as the Melba Finch and Bengalese which will rear the young as their own. Feed as the Pintailed Whydah.

White-Headed Nun

White-Headed Nun   5″   12 cm

Easily kept in a mixed collection where they can be allowed outside during the winter, although of course must be housed at night. As with most small birds they can be kept in a cage but obviously are happier in an aviary. Unfortunately they are difficult to breed, otherwise they are ideal birds for the novice, live long and become very tame. They should be fed as the Black-Headed Nun. Sexes alike.

Indigo Bunting   5″   12 cm

A very colorful bird, although the hen not so brightly colored. Hardy outdoors, the cock having a very pleasant song. They are aggressive towards other birds, especially during the breeding season when they are difficult to breed. If this is attempted they will do best kept to themselves in a planted aviary. Young fed on insects, adult birds fed on canary seed, millets, green food and a few insects.

Indigo Bunting

Cherry Finch

Cherry Finch   4″   11 cm

Small and attractive birds suitable for the novice. They can be kept in a mixed collection of small birds but should be housed during the winter. If breeding is required they should be disturbed as little as possible otherwise they will abandon the nest. Cherry Finches should be fed a staple diet of plain canary seed, millets, spray millet, an occasional maggot and green food. Also insects, insect mixture, sprouted seeds and ants eggs. Sexes similar.

Black-Headed Nun   4"   10 cm

Popular and very easy to keep in a mixed collection in an aviary, although if breeding is wanted they are best kept as a pair alone. Plenty of grass and twigs should be provided as they build a large nest. Chicks should be fed sprouted seeds, seeding grasses and small insects. Adults fed on millets, plain canary seed, spray millet and green food. Sexes similar.

Black-Headed Nun

Java Sparrow

Java Sparrow   5"   12 cm

One of the most familiar and popular cage birds. If well cared for they will live for many years and once acclimatized can be allowed outside during the winter. It is advisable not to keep them with smaller birds. Provide an open-fronted nest-box, plus dry grasses and rootlets with which they will build their nest. Feed the young insect mixture, berries, mealworms, ants eggs, bread and milk etc. The adults fed as Mannikins. Sexes alike.

Magpie Nun   5"   12 cm

One of the larger Mannikins and not so easily obtainable as some other Mannikins. Should not be mixed with smaller birds but can be kept with birds such as Java Sparrows etc. If breeding is desired they should be kept in an aviary to themselves and supplied with lots of twigs, dry grasses and leaves etc. A nest-box with plenty of cover such as shrubs is essential. Feed the young and adults as the Black-Headed Nun. Can be wintered outside. Sexes alike.

Magpie Nun

Nonpareil Bunting   5"   12 cm

A very colorful bunting, although the female is less brightly colored. Can winter outside in a well planted aviary and given housing at night. Color food has sometimes to be given if the male is to keep his bright plumage. A secluded nest-box amongst shrubs provided with mosses, grasses, rootlets and feathers might induce a pair to breed. The young are fed on insects, the adults feeding on canary seed, millets, seeding grasses, green food, and a few insects.

Nonpareil Bunting

Yellow Sparrow

Yellow Sparrow   5"   12 cm

Easy to keep, being hardy outside in a mixed collection with birds of its own size. In a well-planted aviary a pair might breed in a nest-basket or shrub. Chicks feeding on small insects, sprouting seeds, seeding grasses, etc. The adults are very shy during breeding and should not be disturbed. Feed canary seed, millets, millet spray, insects and green food. Sexes similar but the hen is a buff color.

Lazuli Bunting   5"   12 cm

Brightly colored birds, females duller. Once acclimatized they can be mixed with other birds in a planted aviary. The cock has a very pleasant song. These birds are very difficult to breed by the novice. Kept to themselves in a thickly planted aviary a pair might breed nesting in a shrub. Insects are necessary for the young, the adults feeding on canary seed, millets, green food, sprouted seeds and fruit. As with other buntings these birds, although hardbills, require a good supply of insects.

Lazuli Bunting

Pin-Tailed Nonpareil   5"   12 cm

Attractive birds but difficult to acclimatize by the beginner, rather wild and timid. Once acclimatized however are hardy in winter and provided with a planted aviary they should settle down and breed if kept alone, provided with nest-boxes. Can be kept in a mixed collection. Feed on plain canary seed, millets, spray millet, paddy rice, green food and sprouted seeds, and insects for the young. Sexes similar but the hen less colorful.

Pin-Tailed Nonpareil

Tri-Colored Nun

Tri-Colored Nun   4"   10 cm

Simple and easy for the beginner. This is a hardy bird and can be kept in an outside aviary during the winter in a mixed collection. It is difficult to persuade to breed, but if canes or rushes are planted in the aviary a pair might build a nest and breed. Nesting materials as other mannikins. The young are fed on stale soaked bread and sprouted seeds, adults as other Mannikins. Sexes alike.

Spice Bird   4½"   11 cm

Very popular and excellent hardbills for the novice. They are easy to keep and hardy outdoors, but should be housed at night, sometimes roosting in nest-boxes. Can be kept in a mixed collection. Spice Birds (also known as Nutmeg Finches) are difficult to breed but might do so if kept quiet and given a nest-box or basket. The young and adult birds are fed as other Mannikins. Sexes alike.

Spice Bird

Green Avadavat   4"   10 cm

These small birds are rather delicate and difficult for the beginner. Quite hardy once acclimatized but they cannot stand damp and require slightly heated housing during the winter months. They live longer and are healthier if kept in a planted flight. Not a very free breeder but if given quiet conditions will sometimes nest in a shrub or nest basket. Insects must be provided for the young, the adult birds feeding on millets, canary seed, sprouted seeds and insects. Sexes similar, but the hen less colorful.

Green Avadavat

Cordon Bleu

Cordon Bleu   5"   12 cm

A very popular African bird both for color and breeding. Although hardy birds they should not be subjected to extremes of cold and damp. For breeding provide an open-fronted nest-box or basket in an aviary where they will not be disturbed by other birds. Soft grasses and feathers are used for nesting. Insect mixture, small insects, seeding grasses, etc. should be provided for the young, the adults feeding on millets, seeding grasses, insects, canary seed, etc. Sexes similar.

Red Avadavat   4"   10 cm

Males out of the breeding season are a dull color as are the females. Pretty birds and excellent for the beginner, the cock having a pleasant song. They are quite hardy in unheated housing and live longer and keep their bright color if kept in a planted aviary. Can be kept in a mixed collection of small birds where they are likely to breed. Shrubs or basket nests are used for nesting, the chicks being fed on small insects and sprouted seeds. Adults fed on spray millet, seeding grasses, and canary seed, etc.

Red Avadavat

Bengalese

Bengalese 5″ 12 cm

These popular birds are domesticated hybrids and easy for the beginner in their many color variations. Hardy outdoors in a mixed collection or as a cage bird. They breed quite freely in a mixed aviary if nest-boxes and grasses are provided. The feeding requirements are simple being as Mannikins. As with all small birds they should be provided with grit and cuttlefish bone. Clubs and societies exist for the interest of the Bengalese Finch.

Bengalese

African Silverbill

African Silverbill 4″ 10 cm

Easy to keep: outside during the winter when acclimatized, but must be given dry and frost-free housing at night. Can be kept in a mixed collection of other small birds where they will sometimes breed in a nest-box or basket. These should be packed with material to prevent the birds having room to build another nest on top of the previous clutch which they will sometimes do. Adults and young fed as Black-headed Nun. Sexes alike.

Yellow-Winged Sugarbird

Shama

Yellow-Winged Sugarbird 5″ 12 cm

Jewel-like little birds, the hen being olive green. These softbills soon settle down in an aviary or a well-planted conservatory, being hardy. They must be kept clean, given fresh twigs for perches, and water for bathing. Good community birds, but a pair should be kept alone: in a cage if preferred. Nest of rootlets etc. in a shrub or bunch of evergreens. Nestlings fed as adults on maggots, small insects, honey and soft fruit.

Shama 11″ 27 cm

One of the best singing birds and very popular. They must be carefully acclimatized but once this is achieved they prove friendly and very tame, intelligent and hardy. A pair should be kept in an aviary, but the Shama should not be mixed with other birds as they are very aggressive. A nest box or basket should be provided for breeding. The young are fed on insects, the adults allowed liberty in the garden whilst nesting as the Cuban Finch. Feed insect mixture, maggots and green food. The hen is less colorful than the cock.

Golden-fronted
Fruitsucker

Spreo Starling

Spreo Starling   8″   20 cm

With their glossy feathers these birds are exceptionally attractive and popular. The care of these softbills is the same as that required for the Purple Glossy Starling. They should not be put with smaller birds which they might kill. The young birds should be taken away from the parents when independent to avoid conflicts. Very hardy outside where they will sometimes wish to roost. The Spreo should be fed as the Purple Glossy Starling. Sexes alike.

Golden-fronted Fruitsucker   8″   20 cm

These brightly colored Indian softbills should not be allowed outside until fully acclimatized and are better kept in a well planted conservatory or indoor flight, heated during the winter. They are aggressive towards other birds so should not be kept in a mixed collection. Clean conditions and fresh water for bathing must be provided. They must be kept in a quiet position if success in breeding is to be ensured. The nest is usually built in a tall shrub. Feed the young and adults as the Yellow-winged Sugarbird. Sexes similar.

Indian Zosterop

Greater Hill Mynah

Pekin Robin

Indian Zosterop   4"   10 cm

These pretty softbills are excellent for a mixed collection and once acclimatized can be kept outside all winter or in a planted conservatory but cannot stand frost. A pair should be kept to themselves and provided with a planted environment as they will build their nest in a shrub. The young are fed on insects, the adult birds insect mixture, insects, pears, grapes, oranges, and honey. Sexes alike.

Mynah   13"   32 cm

Often kept alone as a cage pet where they become very tame and excellent talkers. If breeding is required a young pair should be housed in a large outside aviary, being very hardy birds. A large nest box is used, the young fed on insects. A large box cage should be provided for a family pet and placed away from draughts. Feed on insect mixture, insects and fruits. Sexes alike.

Pekin Robin   6"   15 cm

An ideal softbill for the novice with its pretty plumage and lovely song. They should be kept as the Zosterops being very hardy active birds enjoying frequent bathing. A breeding pair should be kept alone, nesting in a shrub or nest basket. The young are fed on insects, the adults on a good mixture of foods which include insects, insect mixture, seeds, fruits, green food, etc. Easy to acquire and good mixers, the sexes are similar.

Purple Glossy Starling

Jay

Purple Glossy Starling   9"   22 cm

A popular and beautiful bird that is hardy during the winter. They should not be kept with smaller birds; Jays and large Weavers etc. being suitable companions. A large aviary is required for these birds, a breeding pair should be kept alone, and provided with a large nesting box and nesting materials. The young are fed on various large insects, maggots, etc. Feed the adults on chopped apples, pears, bananas, insect mixture, insects and chopped raw meat. Sexes alike.

Jay   14"   35 cm

Familiar wild birds, becoming tame when kept as pets in an aviary but should not be associated with smaller birds. Given a secluded aviary a pair should breed, nesting in a shrub. The young are fed insects, the adults on fruits, acorns, berries, insects, grain, and raw egg. They are active birds and should not be caged. A pair look very attractive in a planted aviary of native shrubs and trees where single Jays can be mixed with similar birds such as the Magpie and Jackdaw. Sexes alike.

Chinese Painted Quail   5″   12 cm

These birds are valuable in a mixed collection as they provide added interest, only occupying the ground area of the aviary. Clumps of grass should be provided for cover where a pair will usually nest, but no more than one pair of quail should be kept. Larger aggressive birds must not be associated with them. The chicks feed on insects and insect mixture, and should be separated from the parents at four weeks old. Quail are fed a mixed diet of millets, canary seed, mawseed, insects, and green food. The hen is very attractive, being a mixture of browns.

Diamond Dove   8″   20 cm

Like the quail these birds are excellent for a mixed collection of smaller birds where they will breed and are very hardy. They are easily frightened and should not be kept with aggressive birds or other doves. They have a pleasant call note and are very easy to keep. The nest is made in a shallow tray, the young requiring the same food as is provided for the adults. Feed millets, canary seed, maw seed and green food. Sexes similar.

Chinese Painted Quail

Diamond Dove

Index